R🌹SES
R💍NGS
— AND —
REJOICING

ROSES, RINGS & REJOICING

9020 / ISBN 1-55673-173-6

ROSES RINGS AND REJOICING

C.S.S. Publishing Co., Inc.

Lima, Ohio

Editor's Preface

Recently, CSS sent out a call for wedding meditations from the "frontlines" of parish ministry, hoping to discover a few talented writers and creative preachers for inclusion in the present volume. We discovered many. The selection process was difficult and time consuming, but after much deliberation our staff and editors chose the twenty meditations which comprise this collection.

The result, we think, is a fine sampling of the creative endeavors of parish ministers throughout the United States. Our selection includes some of the most talented and creative submissions, and, we hope, enough of a variety so that all readers will be able to find something here of relevance to their own situations.

We have attempted to remove personal references as far as that is possible. It should be noted, however, that each of these meditations was used by a real pastor in a real wedding for a real couple — we think that this is their main strength. It may be necessary, therefore, to make minor adaptations and alterations in the texts as they appear here before the meditations can be used in a new setting for a new couple. It is our hope that these brief sermons will be the basis and inspiration for your own personalized wedding meditations as you meet each new situation.

CSS would like to thank all of those who submitted manuscripts which do not appear here. The collection which you hold in your hands is the creative product of a talented handful of practicing parish pastors, but it is a tribute to all of the dedicated ministers of Christ working and living in local parishes today.

1

*"Kindle In Us The Fire of Your Love . . .
and You Shall Renew the Face of the Earth"*

(Readings: *Genesis 1:26-28, 31; Colossians 3:12-17; John 17:20-26)*

---

the world in which we live
is a fragmented and broken world.
The world created by God to be a beautiful garden,
a paradise for man and woman has become,
for many people,
 a place of hunger and pain,
 a place of war and oppression.

But today,
whatever brokenness lies in the world,
whatever pain discolors our pasts,
begins to fade and dim
in the light of this wedding.

For today, in the marriage of ____ and ____ ,
we see an image of what the world was meant to be.
Today we celebrate a new beginning,
    a new harmony,
    a new bond of love
    as ____ and ____ vow to live,
    for the rest of their lives,
    as husband and wife.

We are happy for them,
but we can also be happy for ourselves
because their marriage is a reminder to us
that God's love does indeed reach into our broken world,
 healing it,
 binding up its wounds,
 bringing it new life.

We all know how love needs to be expressed
if it is to be real.
A gift of flowers,
the words, "I love you"
are simple ways in which
this invisible thing called love
enters into the world of sight and sound.

So it is with God's love.

The sacrament of marriage brings into our world
an image of the otherwise invisible love of God.

In face, ____ and ____ marriage
is, for all who have eyes to see,
a beautiful stained glass window
into which we can gaze
and be reminded of the presence of God who is love.
Today, their love becomes a window
into the very heart of God.

This is how God picks up the broken pieces of the world
and welds them together like chunks of glass
to form an image of "the love beyond all imagining."

____ and ____ , may the colors of your love
be always bright and clear so that God's
light may shine through,
giving beauty and hope
to an otherwise grey and cloudy world.

When we, your family and friends and parish
look at you, we will see more than you realize.
    As you honor and adore each other's
    beauty and talents and strengths,
                we will be reminded
                that such is the reverence with which
                we reverence the Lord
                and the Lord reverences us.

8

As you encourage and support each other
in being all that God calls you to be,
as you discover depths of love and patience
within yourselves,
> the rest of us will recall
> the nurturing love of the Spirit
> who lives in all of us.

As you forgive each other, as you pray together,
as you share your goods with the needy,
in whose faces you find the face of Christ,
> we shall
> in turn see him in you as well . . .

> a face of light and beauty and peace,
> much like your faces today,
> the day on which you unite your love
> with the love of Christ,
a love with strength and beauty
shining forth from your faces of joy,
a love with the power
to renew the face of the earth.

— James M. Schmitmeyer
Mt. St. Mary's Seminary
of the West
Cincinnati, Ohio

2

(Reading: 1 Corinthians 13)

JOURNEYS should be exciting and fun, yet they are also filled with apprehensions and fears. Such is the beginning of the journey we call marriage. We are nervous because we are not sure exactly what we are getting into. We may have mapped out the course for our relationship with another, but we are not 100% sure that the other shares our total expectations. We talked about expectations in relationships several weeks ago and you will recall that I suggested to you, as I will suggest to your family and friends here gathered, that expectations should be re-evaluated on a regular basis. Who you are today will not be who you are next year, either as individuals or as a couple. The willingness to grow and expand your understandings of marriage is critical.

And so the relationship you begin today is not like anything else you have experienced. It is an integral relationship. It will have all elements of living woven within it. There will be joy and sorrow; there will be happiness and frustration; there will be times of ecstacy as well as times of embarrassment and disappointment. In fact with all the varieties of experiences within the relationship we call marriage, I am surprised that it has survived as long as it has. Most people are unwilling to work at making this journey. They would rather bow out of the relationship just when the challenges seem to be the greatest.

We have also talked about how important it is to share with each other on a regular basis how you are feeling. It is critical to the journey that you begin it with the understanding that when your vehicle of travel (called marriage) begins to sputter and malfunction, you stop right away and see a counselor (what might be called a marriage mechanic). To admit that one needs some help is the greatest compliment one can make to a spouse, a friend, or a counselor, because in that admission a person says: "I trust that you will not violate the confession of need I give."

To help work through a situation is to value your relationship. In our counseling I have stressed the necessity for openness with each other and commitment to that which we call marriage. Above all things keep those two ideas at the center of your marriage relationship. Our sharing together was but the beginning of other opportunities for me and others within your family and friend circles to assist you in your marriage. None of us, who have ever been in this journey would fail to admit that it is sometimes a lonely journey, even when you have a spouse to share it with you. But, my dear friends, you need not feel you journey alone.

St. Paul gives us a great piece of advice, but it will mean nothing if we forget that without the Christ at the center of our relationships, we are fallible, we are filled with disappointment, we can hurt another, we can experience pain. Only when the Christ is at the center will we willingly set aside our own expectations and needs in order that another can be fulfilled. That is what Christ did for us and even in our marriages we are challenged to do the same. May God's presence guide you in your journey into oneness in marriage. Amen

— Joseph R. Foster
St. Peter's United
Church of Christ
Amherst, Ohio

3

Once Upon a Time Is Today

---

fROM the days of your childhood, ____ and ____ , you have heard a good many stories which began, "Once upon a time . . . ." Before you embark upon your married life together, moving from this community which has nurtured you and still loves you, I shall make certain you hear one more.

Once upon a time there was a man and a woman. As their lives grew out beyond the boundaries of their separate families, they came to know each other, and as time passed, to love each other. In many ways they were much alike, in other ways very different. In the ways they were alike, they found one another to be delightful companions. In the ways they were different, they were thrilled with the venture of new worlds to be shared. But in all ways, and at every turn in the road, they found love in each other.

One day they decided the world must know this. And so, from city and country, near by and far away, they called together their friends and neighbors and family, that all might know the joy they had found in each other. These people gathered, bringing with them gifts of love and hopes for the future. As they joined with one another on the joyful occasion, as they pondered and prayed, as they reflected on the future before the man and the woman, a few practical souls among them found themselves wondering: can a young man and a young woman find happiness in a place called _(your town)_ ? If there were any among the well-wishers who doubted, surely it was not the man and woman themselves. For them it was not even a question. They knew the answer,

13

because in their love they shared the deep truth of a powerful secret.

They had discovered, you see, that happiness was not tied to any one place but to finding their place. And the place they had selected to begin their life together they would make their own. They would live in it and they would love it. To it they would give their own creative touch. And it would not be just any place but their place, because God had so ordained it. For their God hallowed all places, especially those where a man and a woman live together in love.

They had discovered, too — this man and this woman — that bigness was not a guarantee of happiness. While others may have thought a castle on the Rhine River or a penthouse in a great city was necessary or at least desirable, they had made a more profound discovery that life was more a question of largeness of heart. It was a matter of love. It was a matter of being big enough to say "I love you" or "I'm sorry" or "Let's do something that'll please us both." Where people live that way, no place is ever small.

Let others call it small, they thought; we know far better! They knew that often life is found not in *what* you see, but in *how* you see. And where they went, they would find beauty and goodness in the lives of people, just as they had found beauty and goodness and delight in each other. Some told them, you must go for the gold, the dollars, the money; but they knew a deeper secret. They set their own values which especially celebrated people.

So, at this grand gathering to which they invited family and friends, they sang two songs: one of bright and shining hopefulness because of all God's creation, including their love for each other; and the other of thankfulness for all the saints — the people, especially gathered family and friends — who are part of God's grand network of love in their lives. As they sang, they felt themselves caught up by a great and ancient truth which surpassed all understanding. And in that truth which is love, they would happily live their days.

Once upon a time, ____ and ____ , is today. Your joy is our joy. Your love for each other is full of promise, because love is of God. And that's no fairy tale! Amen

— Glenn L. Borreson
First Lutheran Church
Decorah, Iowa

4

(Reading: 1 Corinthians 13:1-13 KJV)

---

faMILIAR words! Seems as if St. Paul knows what he is talking about! Humanity is best served by individuals who know themselves; that is, their talents, skills, abilities (gifts which they possess and for which they seek to find some function), and service to humankind which is in keeping with their dispositions, temperaments, and strengths.

People sometimes find themselves miscast for their jobs or positions; their qualifications are too high or, sometimes, too low. What qualifies one for marriage? If you should ask anyone, they would probably say, "Love. The ability to give and to receive love, recognize it for what it is, and be able to benefit from it." That would be a very good answer, provided we know what love is.

Remember the story of *Ferdinand, The Bull* by Munro Leaf? Ferdinand was taken into the bullring (as the fighter he was supposed to be) when all he wanted to do was sit and sniff the flowers. The reason he was taken for a fighter was that he was discovered out in the field after being stung by a bee, kicking up his heels and acting very ferocious.

We have to recognize love for what it is — the acceptance of the other person and the commitment to them — whether convenient or not, rewarding or not. This makes love more than a feeling. It casts it in the role of a service, an offering, a sacrifice. It makes it something other than an abstraction. It keeps it with the concrete; a giving and a forgiving.

Listen to what St. Paul says once again on this subject:

Love is patient and kind
Love is not jealous or boastful

Love does not insist on its own way
Love bears all things
Love never ends.

We are all great lovers at heart; and, if you don't believe this, then just ask someone — and they don't have to be a St. Paul. But what this is explaining to us is not the ability to love; it is telling us of love's characteristics, its nature, its consistency, of what it is made. Some hold this to be the greatest scripture on love in the Bible; the greatest, due primarily to the fact that whereas faith and hope have the capacity to take to themselves (that is, to appropriate); love has the ability and the capacity to give and to diffuse.

The nature of love is to give and give again, whether love from the other is forthcoming or not! True love is that tenacity — that characteristic to hold with and to and for the other — in spite of circumstances and conditions. Where is such true love to be found?

Let's read a portion of the text once more and this time insert the name of Christ in the place of love:

CHRIST is patient and kind;
CHRIST is not jealous or boastful. He is not
arrogant or rude.
CHRIST does not insist on his own way. He is not
irritable or resentful. He does not rejoice at
wrong, but rejoices in the right.
CHRIST bears all things, believes all things, hopes
all things, endures all things.

Now, that makes love a reality. By faith we have a Christ — because by his sinless perfect life, his innocent suffering and death, and the power of his resurrection, he has us! To be found by faith in Christ is to be found by love and to be made one in him and in his love. To be found outside of Christ is still to be able to love as a human being but always looking for that certain "something," that fulfillment, that source of eternal satisfying love.

Christ's love in us through faith in him gives and diffuses. It renews us in our minds, our wills, and our affections — and will continue on forever with its capacity to give and forgive.

Now let us insert the names of you as marriage partners in the same portion of Scripture. In the place of that word "love," we will use your names, as two Christian people. Remember, it is the characteristic and the nature of love which is here spoken of, not people or persons or personalities.

_____ and _____ are patient and kind
_____ and _____ are not jealous or boastful, they
are not arrogant or rude,
_____ and _____ do not insist on their own way,
they are not irritable or resentful. They do not
rejoice at wrong but rejoice in the right.
_____ and _____ bear all things, believe all things,
hope all things, endure all things.

God grant us the capacity to love in him every moment of our lives by the power of the Holy Spirit, through the special surrender and sacrifice of Christ Jesus on his Cross for us.

In him we trust. Amen

— Mark Pepoon
Granbury, Texas

19

5

Recently, I saw a cartoon which pointed out to the reader the fact that married people live much longer than those who are single. Based on that fact, the conclusion of the cartoon character was that marriage, then, is simply a means to a slow death.

If that were really true, today would not be an occasion for celebration. But our reason for gathering here today is to rejoice. Today, ____ and ____ make their commitment to each other in the presence of this gathering and in the sight of God. Today we have all come to this place to share with ____ and ____ this special day. Today, we have gathered together, and the very thing which has brought us together is love.

If you look up the word "love" in the dictionary, you will find as many as 102 different definitions. The love which has brought us together today, though, is a very special kind of love. The love in which ____ and ____ unite is not a sensual, physical kind of love. It has nothing to do with the senses or with the instincts. Rather, it is a kind of moral love; a love which conveys the idea of goodwill and friendship. It is a thoughtful love with a spiritual quality; in a sense, a sort of reverence which indicates what our attitude toward God and toward each other ought to be.

Pearl Buck has described this love as a love which "cannot be forced, cannot be coaxed and teased. It comes out of Heaven, unmasked and unsought." And, as we heard a moment ago, the apostle Paul describes it as a love which is "patient and kind; a love which is not jealous or boastful . . . [It] bears all things, believes all things, hopes all things, endures all things." It is a love which is truly special.

21

The love which brings a man and a woman to this place, to this special event, begins as a cooperative friendship, and is first and foremost a friendship. It is a relationship which is characterized by a profound sense of bonding which goes much deeper than any sort of physical attraction. It is a bond which unites two as one in faith and loyalty and love toward each other and toward the One who has brought these two together. It is a bond which draws each person out of the loneliness and isolation of a self-centered life and turns the gaze of each toward the other. It is a bond which draws these two individuals into a oneness of faith, hope, and love that nothing in life or death could ever destroy. It is the bond which is spoken of by the writer of Ecclesiastes: the bond of two individuals who will have good reward for their work; who will lift up the other after a fall; who will keep each other warm as they live together instead of alone. And it is a bond which cannot be broken when it becomes the interwoven threefold cord of the love of a man, the love of a woman, and the love of God.

The love which brings us, and especially brings the two of you here today is indeed a special kind of love. It isn't a love which makes everything all better, which takes away the irritations, and erases all the bad habits. This special kind of love is not a love which keeps everything happy when both are tired, or when the money is tight, or when the house or the job or any other aspect of life isn't just the way you want it. This special love which brings the two of you together today is a love which does not consist of gazing constantly at each other, but rather consists of looking outward together in the same direction.

_____ and _____ , today you make your commitment to abide with each other in a faith which is the assurance of things hoped for, the conviction of things not seen, and is strengthened by the closeness of another individual who wishes to share life with you. Today, you make your commitment to abide in a hope which searches for new beginnings and new possibilities, and which seeks to accomplish as two who are united what

22

could never be accomplished by one. Today, you make your commitment to abide in a love that crowns and completes your relationship with a spirit that burns with a steadier flame than any simple romantic passion. And the greatest of this is love, your love, founded in Jesus Christ, which puts the two of you in a place more holy than the interior of any church.

So ____ and ____ today as you become one in the presence of this gathering and in the sight of God, through the power of this very special love, let me close by assuring you that if it is true that marriage is simply a means to a slow death, then what a way to go. Amen

— Jeffrey A. Nelson
Lyster Lutheran Church
Nelson, Wisconsin

6

(Reading: 1 Corinthians 12:31b—13:13)

BeƒoRe the altar of our Lord we come together.
We stand — hand in hand —
and wish to hear the words which God would say.
We wish for joy and life and happiness
His voice we hear proclaim,
"I will show you the most excellent way."

the most excellent way is the way of love.
Not a love of human urge and pleasure,
But the love from God above.
This is love, the love beyond all measure.

an individual may speak,
with words of most convincing logic,
with words of arguments persuasive,
with words as honey sweetly dripping from the lips,
but those words
without the love of God embodied
are but clanging gongs
and harsh disharmony.

In the marriage covenant
the most excellent way is the way of love.
In your marriage covenant
let the words which are spoken
be the words which are taken
from the way of God's love:
the most excellent way.

25

as children of the heavenly Father
you have listened to his Word.
You have tried to live in honor and obedience
as you have gone into the world.
You may know his will,
and you may have the faith,
faith to move the highest mountains.
But that faith and wisdom,
without the love of God directed,
is but nothing:
a void of empty lonely thought.

In the marriage covenant,
the most excellent way is the way of love.
In your marriage covenant,
let your wisdom and your faith
be centered and guided
in the way of God's love:
the most excellent way.

you could give up all the wealth that you have,
your money and name,
possessions and fame.
You could die for your faith,
but it would count for no gain.
For shed without love
these efforts and deeds
are but feeble and shallow
devoid of true life,
no meaning indeed.

In the marriage covenant
the most excellent way is the way of love.
In your marriage covenant
let the deeds that you do,
the gifts that you give,
be given in love —
the love from our God:
it is the most excellent way.

this way — the way of God's love
is so full and so great.
When life is lived from the way of above,
that love does our very existence penetrate.
We find ourselves transformed and transported,
from things small and petty distorted;
to things which are holy and hopeful and true.
No longer the envy, the boasting, the pride.
No longer the rudeness, self-seeking, or anger.
Now comes the patience, the kindness, the truth.
And also the trusting, the hope, and the future.
For in this love,
the love of our Savior,
our future is safe and forever secure.

In the marriage covenant
the most excellent way is the way of God's love.
In your marriage covenant
let God's love overwhelm you
and in joy unify you.
God's love after all
is the most excellent way for you.

As you stand here this day
with promise and honor
you pledge to each other:
faithfulness, devotion, and love.
Look to the future together
and what do you see it to be?
The things of our doing,
our thoughts and our wisdoms,
our deeds and our ways,
these are the things
which cannot help but pass away.
But the way of our Lord,
the way of that love,
is steady and sure,
for then, and for now, and for times to come still.

27

for the way of God's love is the most excellent way.
In marriage that love is the best way of all.
And life in such love is today
full of promise —
potential immense and tremendous.
God's love is the most excellent way.

now our vision is dim,
mere shadows we see,
of life in such love,
of what we can be.
We feel so young,
inadequate, not sure.
We struggle like children
to be faithful and pure.
We live in his love
but it's like we're half there.
It's imperfect and broken,
this life we live here.
God's promise to us,
in this way of his love,
is that life will be whole
when we come to his home high above.

In the marriage covenant,
the most excellent way is the way of God's love.
In your marriage covenant,
let your life lived together
be centered and ordered
by grace and forgiveness
from Christ freely given,
in hope and sure promise
of glorious heaven.
This way of God's love is
the most excellent way for you.

the way of God's love,
three words summarize it:
faith, and hope, and love.
One word typifies it:
The greatest of these
is none other than love.
In his love he has given,
unlimited promise.
For what God has given
is Christ's death and life for us.
This is his most excellent way
the way of his love to us.

So joining together
in vows of commitment
is centered in love,
God's love and fulfillment.
These two will be one,
they will be faithful we pray.
For God in his love
has shown unto them
the most excellent way.

— Joel W. Kreger
St. Luke Lutheran Church
Nora Springs, Iowa

7

love and fear

(Reading: 1 John 4:18)

---

the verb or the noun "love" occurs in twenty-six of the 105 verses of First John. In all cases, it is the familiar root *agape*. The leading idea is that God is love by nature and that he revealed this by sending Christ into the world. (4:9) We are not love by nature, and therefore God loved us first. The measure of this love was the death of Christ on our behalf (3:16) and therefore the Father could call us children. (3:1) This makes possible our own response of love and so if we abide in love, we abide in God. (4:16) The writer does not allow us to remain misty-eyed over love, however, for he gives sharp content to the word. We love God by keeping his commandments. (5:3) We are to *do* rather than to *feel*. We are to believe in Christ *and* to love one another. (3:23) There are teeth placed in the command to love. If we do it, we are in the light (2:10); but if we don't, we live in the realm of death. (3:14) We cannot give equal billing to the world, for love of the world excludes the love of God. (2:15) If we won't love the brother whom we have seen, then we lie if we say that we love God whom we have not seen. (4:20)

We are commanded to love the brothers and sisters in the Lord in specific ways. We are to love them in deeds and not in pious words. (3:18) We are not to close our hearts to one in need. (3:17) As Christ gave his life for us, we are to be willing to give our life for another. (3:16) The result of this kind of love is confidence to face the Last Judgment (4:17) because love casts out fear. (4:18)

The idea of commanded love, which is stressed in this epistle, is alien to us, for we consider love to be an emotion. In

31

Latin the heart came to be a symbol for emotions in general and love in particular, and found its way into our Valentine's Day cards. The Greeks knew that an emotion provides at best a slippery motivation for action, however, and they used the lower intestines as their comparable symbol. When the New Testament uses "heart" as a symbol it means the entire mind — the memory, the logical faculty, and the will. There may be feeling there, and we hope there is, but it is not pre-requisite to loving in the biblical sense. If our response of love is a matter of the will, then it is dependable over the long haul. When a man and woman fall "in love" the sky-rockets explode. When they decided to form a family before God, however, much more is involved than the sky-rockets. It is the will, and not emotion, which maintains a family over the years. They can continue loving even when they don't feel like it. First John does not use this particular verb of the love of man and wife, but in Ephesians 5:25 husbands and wives are to love each other *as* Christ loves the church. This had better be more consistent than the vagaries of our emotions, or else our future in Christ is not as secure as the New Testament claims.

It is appropriate to place ＿＿＿＿ 's and ＿＿＿＿ 's love for each other within the larger context of the interlocking areas of concern for God and the brothers and sisters in Christ. The essence of a marriage is their decision that they can live more effectively together than they can separately. In this chapel today we recognize three parties to this contract — God, the two of them, and the rest of us representing Christian society as a whole.

Listen to the words of 1 John 4:18: "There is no fear in love, but perfect love casts out fear. For fear has to do with punishment, and he who fears is not perfected in love (RSV)." The point of this verse is that love and fear are incompatible. They do not mix any better than do oil and water. Love is the approach to the other out of desire for the good of the other. Fear is a shrinking away because of expected punishment. We cannot approach and hide in fear at the same time — to God, to the spouse, or to the brothers and sisters in Christ. Fear breeds suspicion and isolation and therefore hinders the growth of love. Either the fear or the love must win.

The "fear" of this verse is related to what is variously translated as "torment" or "punishment" or "judgment." The word originally means to cut back the growth of a tree or a bush by pruning. From this, it comes to mean cutting back bad behavior by corrective discipline. Parents and children train each other in this way, as do husband and wife, and so God corrects us. This word does not indicate punishment for its own sake, but corrective discipline. It is, therefore, a positive rather than a negative idea. When it is associated with fear, the fear is of rejection. The point of the verse is that if we *love* God, then we know that it is discipline intended to bring us closer to him. If we *fear* God, by contrast, we see it as ultimate rejection. For this reason the word in Matthew 25:46, its only other occurrence in the New Testament, means punishment in hell. The more we love God, however, the more we understand that God's purpose is discipline rather than rejection. Because of this, love conquers fear, but fear shows that the love is not yet perfect. In the same way, ____ and ____ will find it necessary to discipline each other as they live together. If they see it as punishment, they will fear each other and pull apart. But if, instead, by their love, they will see it as discipline, they will increasingly draw together.

This is the growth which is implied in 1 John 4:18. The better our love for God, the less the fear. This better love for God then allows us a better love for each other in Christ and for the two of them within the marriage bond. It is significant that love, rather than courage, is what conquers fear. We cannot be brave by an effort of will, but we can make a deliberate decision to love. The love of ____ and ____ for God has not yet been made perfect. Their love for the brothers and sisters is not yet perfect. And their love for each other is not yet perfect. But they have made a start in all three directions. There is, no doubt, still a remaining tinge of fear in all three relationships, but their on going life in the Spirit of God tips the

33

balance more and more on the side of love. At the end, our prayer for them is that they demonstrate that "there is no fear in love, but perfect love casts out fear."

— Charles E. Wolfe
Hampstead, Maryland

8

Entreat me not to leave you. Where you go — I will go.

(Reading: Ruth 1:16-17)

---

the ingredients of a lasting relationship include this commitment of similar values: living/lodge, people/friends — family, God/ultimate reality, death/death. The relationship is entered into with the quality of permanence. This implies the need to create a meaningful marriage, to promise to work at growing in love.

These two have accepted the gift of a love that makes two come together as one. The love poem from Paul's letter to the Corinthians emphasizes patience, kindness, non-irritability, control of jealousy, boasting, arrogance, resentfulness. These are all qualities of interaction between persons. As ideals they confront us with objectives to grow in graciousness, respect, mutual supportiveness. Our need for divine forgiveness accompanies our aspirations that somehow the climate of our love will nurture the growth of these qualities among us.

The contemporary words of Kahil Gibran, (*The Treasure of Kahil Gibran*) "Love is the only freedom in the world because it so elevates the spirit that the laws of humanity do not alter its course," also confront them. ____ and ____ have found this freeing quality in each other's presence. Some insight to the self occurs when we are valued, treasured, loved. Some new encounter with untouched feelings, ideas, abilities re-creates us. The partnership becomes more than the sum of two persons uniting. It is the budding of new risks of self and meaning, the discovery of beauty, truth, and goodness.

One couple put it this way: "This is the beginning of the achievement of common goals, the desire to provide a loving home for our family, sharing and growing together as individuals building a marriage that is mutually enriching.''

It is my privilege to share in the public celebration of this union of ____ and ____ . Each of you is fortunate to receive one who shares your faith, hope, and love. Be gentle to each other.

May I close with this word collage of love which I share with you from my thoughts:

Love is a gift!
When we respond to it sensitively . . .
it rises within us
like the dawn
or declines with the dusk
to grant rest . . .

It may enhance our best,
or make us smug in possessiveness —
Unless it is shared and watered,
it will wither and crumble . . .

most delicately we need
to discover the gift
to open it without selfishness
to allow its fulfillment to
make us free.

Love is more than
a feeling —
greater than my thoughts
more simple than nature
more complex than
the computer brain —

yet it comes
when needed
like sunshine
or refreshing rain.

— Robert A. Kramer
Stonybrook United Methodist
Church
Gahanna, Ohio

9

---

the opening sentence of *The Order for the Service of Marriage* is one of the most starkly beautiful in the English language:

> *Dearly beloved, we are gathered together here in the sight of God, and in the presence of these witnesses, to join together this man and this woman in holy matrimony; which is an honorable estate, instituted of God, and signifying unto us the mystical union which exists between Christ and his Church; which holy estate Christ adorned and beautified with his presence in Cana of Galilee.*

What a lovely combination of words! How dynamic are their expression! How inclusive their compass! Surely Archbishop Cranmer, who in 1549 edited *The Book of Common Prayer*, from which these words derive, was not only a man of special sanctity but also of peculiar genius. *Consider how they first remind us of who is present:* we are gathered here in the sight of God, as well as in the presence of several witnesses. This is no social nicety which we observe this afternoon. The law of the land certainly will be fulfilled and social amenities surely will be observed, but the solemnization of holy matrimony is much more than that. We are participating in a high and holy service of worship. The people of God have assembled themselves together in a place set aside by common consent for divine worship. The church, the people of God, the Body of Christ have come together to participate in an action of mutual concern, and as our Lord did truly remind us, "Where two or three are gathered together in my name, there am I in the midst of them." (Matthew 18:20) God himself is truly present at this moment, actively participating with us in our corporate action, taking our mortal words and human actions and clothing them with eternality and divinity. We are to be wtinesses to a covenantal action, the establishment of a new relationship between three persons — _____ , _____ , and God. It is a relationship that is intended to be everlasting, a relationship of love and hope and given-ness. It is to be a holy relationship because it is to be established in the presence of God.

Secondly, we note that matrimony is "an honorable estate, instituted by God, and signifying unto us the mystical union which exists between Christ and his Church." *These words remind us that marriage is not a tradition of humanity's inauguration but of God's institution.* Holy matrimony is the most ancient of all the ordinances of God, the first command uttered by the Lord God after the creation of humankind. The venerable scribe who first preserved the *Genesis* story recorded that "God created man in his own image, in the image of God he created him; male and female he created them. And God blessed them, and God said to them, 'Be fruitful and multiply, and fill the earth and subdue it; . . .' " (Genesis 1:27-28)

There is divine purpose in marriage as well as human purpose. The two go hand-in-hand; they augment and complete one another, even as Christ and his church augment and complete one another. This fulfillment of both divine and human purpose is what St. Paul means when he describes it as "the fulness of him who fills all in all." (Ephesians 1:23) Marriage was ordained to effect a mutuality of society, of help, of comfort, of fulfillment between man and woman, between humankind and God. Heaven and earth meet in a truly Christian marriage. Each partner is enabled to help the other on to a more wholesome life, a holier life because of their awareness of the abiding presence of God in their union. At the same time, both partners are equipped by God's grace to more fully realize and appreciate the material joys of life which God intends for all of his creatures. Dante, in his classic poem, *Paradise*, tells of how he was aware of his ascent into the high plains of Paradise only because it was first mirrored in the face of his beloved Beatrice. So it is marriage ordained by God — and many a home can trace the upward ascent of one partner because of the beauty and holy influence of the other partner.

Finally, the opening sentence prompts us to remember that, "Christ adorned and beautified (marriage) with his presence in Cana of Galilee." The account of this wedding is found in the second chapter of *The Gospel of John:* "On the third day there was a marriage at Cana in Galilee, and the mother of Jesus was there; Jesus also was invited, with his disciples." (John 2:1-2)

What lovely images confront us in those two verses! A Jewish wedding was an occasion of great joy and hilarious festivity. All who were friends of both families were invited, as well as all the relatives. And John emphasized, "Jesus also was invited." He was there, he was wanted, he was an honored guest. No question arose as to whether he would "fit in." He was there with his friends, enjoying their company. Our Lord was no severe, austere killjoy. He was a human, a whole human as well as a holy human, and he enjoyed life to the fullest. He shared in the joy and happiness of the wedding because he had been invited — and it takes no large imagination to hear his hearty laughter and to see his warm smile as he wished the bride and groom happiness and health in their new life together.

But something else occurred at that long-ago wedding. There, before the wedding company, he performed the first of his miracles. They ran out of wine for the guests, and acting on the faith of his mother, Jesus turned water into wine. It was a little need that Jesus met there, but Jesus met it even as he meets us in all of our weightier needs. In a humble Galilean home, at a village girl's wedding, Jesus Christ, the eternal Son of God, first revealed the power of God which rested upon him — because he cared. The happiness of that young couple, whoever they were, mattered to him. It was to save a family from hurt and humiliation that Jesus first revealed his power. It was in sympathy, in kindness, in understanding

41

that he acted. He had been invited to the wedding — and by his presence and through his gracious action, he "adorned and beautified" it. It was at a wedding — a wedding with many similarities to the one soon to be consummated here — that Jesus performed "the first of his signs . . . at Cana in Galilee, and manifested his glory; and (because he did) his disciples believed in him." (John 2:11)

In the presence of God is a marriage initiated; by obedience to the will of God is a marriage sustained; and through faith in Jesus as Lord is a marriage "adorned and beautified," or as we would say, made Christian. These three principles are found all in one sentence, the sentence with which *The Order for the Service of Marriage* begins.

And by these principles — and these alone — does a Christian marriage endure.

In the name of the Father and of the Son and of the Holy Ghost. Amen

> — Raymond W. Gibson, Jr.
> Campus Minister, Union College
> Barbourville, Kentucky

10

____ and ____:

the author of First Peter wrote (as we read it in The Living Bible:

And now this word to . . . you: You should be . . . a happy family, full of sympathy toward each other, loving one another with tender hearts and humble minds. Don't repay evil for evil. Don't snap back to those who say unkind things about you. Instead, pray for God's help for them, for we are to be kind to others, and God will bless us for it.

(1 Peter 3:8-9)

____ , this is the third time that you have stood before me in a unique relationship. When you were nearly four months old, your parents held you as I baptized you in the Christian faith. Thirteen years later, at this altar, you stood alone as I placed my hand upon your head and confirmed you in the Christian faith. Today you and ____ stand together, and I stand before you again, this time to unite you in marriage.

If I could summarize the words of Scripture concerning marriage, the prayers of your parents, the good wishes of your friends, and the blessing of your pastors, it would be in three simple but profound truths.

First, *be lovers all your life.* We all know that marriage is not merely an adventure of romantic love. Only fools believe that marriage is an endless series of emotional thrills. Yet as you go about your daily tasks, keep romance alive by the little things you do throughout the day. Be courteous to each other at all times. Respect each other's feelings and thoughts,

43

T. HUG.

ideas and dreams. Express appreciation freely. Build one another up. Never let a day go by without saying "I love you." Say it not only in words, but with a wink in public when no one is looking, a squeeze of the hand, or a loving touch as you are hurrying about the house.

A happy marriage never develops by accident. It is cultivated from the day you are married until the day that God calls one of you to his eternal home. Work as diligently and persistently for "togetherness" as you have during your engagement. Be lovers all your life.

Second, *be honest with each other*. Avoid that day when you cannot be open and frank, honest and truthful with one another. When there are lies between husband and wife, when there is unfaithfulness, and when there is deceit, the bloom of marriage begins to fade. Live one life together and make that an open book which you both share.

Being honest means also listening to each other. You may not always agree, but each should respect the other's right to their own thoughts. Hear what the other person is trying to say. We need to talk to each other, but we also need to listen to each other. We grow in an honest relationship not only by being truthful ourselves, but also by letting the other person be truthful. Don't wear masks before each other; let your partner be the person God wanted him or her to be. Respect each other's right to fulfill God's intended destiny.

Third, *be one in worship*. I am always troubled when a couple shares a common home, when they sleep, eat, work, bank, shop, and play together but cannot worship God together. There is unity in worship. Together, you need the blessings of God more than anything else in the world. How beautiful it is when husband and wife worship together on the Lord's Day.

The poet said that we need to hitch our wagon to a star, but I say that we need to link marriage with God. Ask God to come into your home. Make God a part of all that you do.

Let God be the senior partner in your marriage. When you do that, your marriage which is now being made on earth, will be sealed in heaven. May God bless you richly in your years together.

— O. Garfield Beckstrand, II
Trinity Lutheran Church
Rockford, Illinois

11

Then the Lord God said, "It is not good that the man should be alone; I will make him a helper fit for him . . . Therefore a man leaves father and mother and cleaves to his wife, and they become one flesh.

(Reading: Genesis 3:18, 24)

Dear _____ and _____ :

I am sure that the wish of all this afternoon, not only yourselves, but also your parents and certainly our Lord, is that you together might begin this day to live lives of fullness and happiness. And what each of us would want to share most with you (even more than any gift, present, token, or tribute) would be a formula for this happiness. A prescription which suggests itself to us on this occasion is one taken from Holy Scripture. It is a prescription with three ingredients.

1. *Remember that no one is perfect.* No matter how deeply you love your partner, you will at times (in the future) act selfishly, speak out in anger, hurt, and perhaps alienate. The Bible reminds us: "If we say that we have no sin we deceive ourselves and the truth is not in us." (1 John 1:8) And your partner may hurt and fail you, too. Many marriages are unhappy or insecure because one of the partners fails to allow for mistakes in his or her spouse. But God who "remembers that we are dust" (Psalm 103:14) does not expect us to build our marriage on human attempts to appear perfect, or on expectations that our spouse is flawless.

The second principal then follows the first.

2. *Realize that forgiveness is a way of life.* Forgiveness is God's way of life for his children who realize they are sinners, admit their need, and receive pardon of sins through Jesus

47

Christ, who paid the price on the cross to atone for all our transgressions. The Bible reminds us to be: "Forgiving [of] one another, even as God, for Christ's sake has forgiven us." (Ephesians 4:32) If there is forgiveness in your life, almost anything can be dealt with successfully and overcome, regardless of how great the handicaps or hardships.

And the last principal is:

3. *Renew your commitment.* The Bible tells us that marriage is a commitment of love. In marrying, a man and a woman "leave and cleave." They leave their parents* and cleave to each other (Matthew 19:5) to commit themselves to each other for life. This total commitment to each other is the changeless mark of Christian marriage.

By renewing this commitment of love (not only in thought and sentiment, but in word and action) on a daily basis, and by following the principles of 1. recognizing the human-ness of each other, and 2. living in forgiveness, you can set out together in life to experience more and more what God intended for all marriages when he said that the "two shall become one." With these principles you can experience the harmony in marriage which God intended, and you can be a blessing to each other as well as to those around you. Amen

— Dennis A. Kastens
  Good Shepherd Lutheran Church
  Collinsville, Illinois

---

*They leave their *pasts* (vs. parents) . . . *Used when a previously married person is nuptially united.*

12

_____

___ and ___ ,

the decision which you have made is among the most important you will ever make. Like all choices, it is made in the context of human uncertainty. It is a faith decision. There are no guarantees that the way ahead for you will be smooth and straight. There is no promise that the commitment you make so joyously today will be easy to maintain. On the contrary, the promises which you make to one another will require constant attention and continuing commitment. Just as your love has not begun and does not end with this service of marriage, the relationship to which you publicly commit yourself today is an ongoing, living bond between you. The days ahead will bring changes in your lives. You will change as individuals and your relationship with one another will change. Yet, if you are faithful to the commitments which you make before God and us this day, the changes which take place will deepen your love for one another and enable you to know better the One through whom the mystery of your love has happened.

One of the most precious gifts we can offer to you is the assurance born out of the experience of countless witnesses that true love and faithfulness never come to an end. Hear the words of St. Paul to the church at Corinth concerning love:

Love is always patient and kind; it is never jealous; love is never boastful or conceited; it is never rude or selfish; it does not take offense, and is not resentful. Love takes no pleasure in other people's sins but delights in the truth; it is always ready to excuse, to trust, to hope and to endure whatever comes. Love does not come to an end. There are three things that last: faith, hope and love, but the greatest of these is love.

— Scott Campbell
E. Longmeadow, Massachusetts

13

Oh, Lord, we come to you today to praise you and to make ourselves available for your blessing. ____ and ____ have commited their lives to each other. They want to serve each other and You. Today we pray, help them to receive the love that You will give; help them to know and to live the peace that is Your peace; help them to know the confidence and security of this relationship with You.

In Your Spirit, Oh Lord, the issues of each day will be growing experiences, and togetherness will be most complete. You will make us of one spirit as we maintain our own persons. You will be our Lord as we both laugh and cry together.

We say thank you for the blessings of this moment. Our future prayers of praise and need will be to You and we will present ourselves in Jesus' name. Amen

The most beautiful experience in life is finding that one who makes you feel whole because you feel a completeness with each other.

We have come together today because ____ and ____ have found this completeness with each other and with God and wish to be joined by God in holy marriage.

Love is a soul quality, not of the senses, but of the mind, and is therefore an eternal quality. It knows none of the negative qualities of selfishness, envy, or jealousy.

Love cannot be possessed; therefore, ask not for love, but give it — for in giving love, you are giving yourself in all you do. This is the one principle of love.

Love is like the ascent of a mountain. It comes nearer, ever nearer to you as you go nearer to it. Meeting all of life's

51

challenges with a loving attitude keeps romance bright and fresh.

All the seemingly unpleasant chores are in reality chores of loving service. They give us the opportunity to serve each other — and to serve each other is our great purpose in life.

True love is the expression of the spiritual, mental, and physical harmony which grows out of deep respect, one for the other. Love, the surest foundation of all, provides strength on which true marriage rests. Its bonds create harmony, its practice draws the smile of God.

We have come to participate in a service which will nurture life. Marriage is the embodiment of the fundamental freedom of every human being, the freedom to love. Such then, is marriage: the choosing to love without reservation, the choice to risk oneself, to commit one's life to caring for another.

_____ and _____ , in coming to the marriage altar you are performing an act of absolute faith, believing in one another to the end. But marriage is not only living for each other; it is two uniting to serve God. God is joining you together. He will seal your covenant with his. Thus, you will be the instruments of his will. You, in your freedom, have joyously responded to God's love within you. He is creating something beautiful out of your love. Thank God for his love — his first, then yours.

Marriage is more than your love for each other; it is God's holy ordinance; it is his act — not yours. By the will of God you belong to each other as long as you both shall live.

Marriage is a holy covenant between two people pledged to love each other, trust each other, and face life together. Marriage speaks of separation — separation from selfish aims, separation from personal gain. And marriage speaks of unity — unity in purpose, unity in responsibility, unity in joy. These, now two, shall be one.

There is no relationship which is stronger, yet more delicate, than this union to which you have now come to commit yourselves. The vows you take today will last for life. There will be days of adjustments and periods of change and growth. But love that binds you today will bring joy far surpassing any problems you may encounter in your life together.

> — Randall S. Lehman
> Church of the Brethren
> Muskegan, Michigan

14

Willful Love

(Readings: 1 Corinthians 13:1-7, 13—14:1a)

The scripture for this wedding service is a favorite passage for many people. It is one which is especially appropriate before the vows of marriage, because it speaks of love, not for the moments of the ceremony, but for the months leading to this hour and the years following this day. It speaks of love for the long-haul and the tough times.

The love encouraged in this passage has nothing to do with the soft lens photo of a couple in wedding clothes gazing at a pond with graceful swans, followed by a sentimental greeting card verse. It has nothing to do with romantic songs or champagne toasts. This scripture, rather, has everything to do with real life. This is part of a long letter that St. Paul wrote to the church in Corinth. He was writing to them because word had come to him that they were quarreling among themselves. Paul knew how destructive such prolonged controversy could be to the church and how confusing and distasteful it appeared to those outside the church. So he counseled them on the specifics of their quarrel, climaxing his counsel with this hymn of love just read.

The love which Paul extols is a love which acknowledges that conflict will occur in close relationships. This love which Paul proclaims is a willful love — one which wills good, not evil for others. This love is a willful decision to exercise tolerance in spite of living with the same petty annoyances, not of a few weeks but of many years. This love is a willful commitment to steadfastly, caringly support one another through the unbearable. This love is a willful pledge to enjoy and have joy in one another.

_____ and _____ you already have some experience of this willful love, not only through the example of your parents, but also in your love for one another thus far. One other very important thing needs to be said about the kind of love Paul describes. It does not happen through our own effects. It is a mysterious gift of God. You need only to be open and willing to act out that gift. Paul is clear, and the story of Christian faith is clear, that the source of this kind of love is Jesus Christ. Your relationship with Christ will be the key to having this willful love present in your marriage.

The quality of your marriage can be a testimony not just to your love, but to the love of God. It can be a beacon of hope for others and a safe harbor of faith and love for yourselves. So, I challenge you and encourage you with the help of God to make this willful love your aim. Amen

— Lynne M. Meyers
Prairie Dell Presbyterian Church
Shannon, Illinois

15

Marriage is built on five Cs. That's right. There are five words, encompassing five concepts, beginning with the letter C, that help to form the basis for a Christian marriage. ____ and ____ , I hope you will let the following words be vehicles for strength in your marriage bond.

The first word is *Christ*. Yes, Jesus Christ is the rock upon which your marriage must be based. He's the building block, the corner stone, as it were. He gladdened the wedding feast at Cana with his presence. You will do well to found your marriage upon Jesus Christ. Remember your own personal devotional practices. Will you have table grace at meals, prayer, and a daily time of devotions together? Remember that your hope for this marriage is built on Christ and that all other ground is sinking and, i.e., it goes for nothing.

The second word is *caring*. By this I really mean love and compassion and kindness. The motto for the Hallmark card people is, "When you care enough to send the very best." Well, we have a Hallmark God, one who "cared enough to send the very best." And that very best was his own Son, Jesus. Strive to emulate his love, his compassion, and his kindness of spirit, which he showed toward others. Be considerate and thoughtful of each other.

The third word is *communication*. My, how many marriages have broken down simply because the couple has ceased to talk with each other. This is all-important. When we forgo prayer and a time of daily communion with God, we find ourselves drawing further away from him. The same is true with human beings. We need to talk, to communicate, in order to maintain a closeness of feeling and relationship together. I know that you will be busy and there will always be a hundred other things that you could be doing. But even if it's only for fifteen minutes at the close of the day, please share with each other something of what has gone on with you that day: your hurts and your joys, your plans and your dreams. As long as you can communicate, there will always be hope for a stronger marriage.

A fourth word is *conflict*. It may seem strange to you that this word is included. Yet I have found that many marriages break down simply because they do not know how to handle conflict constructively. You will have conflict. No two people can live together as closely as you two are going to live together, without some conflict. So what if you disagree or have different opinions? You're human. This is normal. The important thing is to be able to talk your conflicts out, to talk things through, to try to better understand each other. If you will work through your conflicts, rather than ignoring them or refusing to talk about them, you will find that they will render your marriage stronger than ever.

The final word is *counseling*. By all means, if problems or concerns seem to be getting too much for you and you are not sure you can handle them together, ask some professional outside help. It may be your pastor or a professional marriage or family counselor. Often, an objective observer, looking at your relationship from the outside, can see things which you, the married couple, cannot see, simply because you are too close to the situation with so many emotions and feelings involved. Too often people will seek counseling as a last resort or after the decision has already been made to separate and possibly dissolve the marriage. Remember that seeking help is a sign of strength, not weakness. Seek God's help and his guidance through prayer and meditation, and God can use others as his instruments to bring about healing and wholeness in your marriage relationship.

Well, there you have it, the five Cs for marriage. Think about them. For remember that the way you handle these five important areas in your married life may well determine whether you have a good marriage or a poor one, or a marriage at all.

_____ and _____ may Christ's loving presence strengthen and enrich your marriage. Amen

> — Hollis A. Miller
> Zion Lutheran Church
> Lexington, South Carolina

16

The Mystery of Marriage

It seems like everyone enjoys a good mystery. In bookstores and libraries, whole sections are devoted to mystery books. Authors like Ed McBain and Robert Ludlum can hardly keep up with readers' demands. On television, the most popular shows are mysteries like *Hardcastle and McCormick*, *Cagney and Lacy*, and *Crazy Like a Fox*.

This evening, as we celebrate the love that ____ and ____ have found with one another, we come to share in a mystery. The writer of the Book of Proverbs tells us this:

Three things are too wonderful for me;
Four I do not understand;
The way of an eagle in the sky,
The way of a serpent on a rock,
The way of a ship on the high seas,
And the way of a man with a maiden.

(Proverbs 30:18-19)

The Apostle Paul also speaks of marriage as a mystery when he writes:

For this reason a man shall leave his father and his mother and be joined to his wife, and the two shall become one. This is a great mystery, and I take it to mean Christ and the Church.

(Ephesians 5:31-32)

And so tonight; the handsome tuxedo, the lovely dress, the beautiful flowers are telling us how special tonight is. For when I see you at the grocery, you are not dressed like this. And when I see you at the store, you never wear a tuxedo. But tonight is special, as we celebrate the mystery of love, a love that is linked to the mystery of Christ and his church — a love that depends not just on you, but on the grace and power and unity we have with Christ and his people.

In his power, God created you man and woman.
In his wisdom, God brought you together.
In his grace, God will make you one.

In the mysterious future, in the days ahead, you have each other and Christ; to have and to hold, for better or for worse, for richer for poorer, in sickness and in health, to love and to cherish, till death do you part. Out of all the people in the world, you will now have each other. Marriage is a mystery, so profound that you will never exhaust its meaning; so deep and complex, that each day will be a new adventure.

In the future _____ , _____ will not always be wearing a tuxedo. You will see him in a ratty looking T-shirt, with stubble on his chin glued to a football game on television or meticulously scrubbing pots and pans in the kitchen and you'll think "what have I gotten myself into?" And _____ , _____ will not always look as lovely as she does tonight. You will see her with a runny nose, grey bags under her eyes, and half the garden on her clothes, and you'll think "Is this the woman I married?" But that's the mystery. Marriage is more than tuxedos and lovely dresses and beautiful flowers and a candlelit church; it is the mystery of two becoming one, and the mystery of Christ and his church.

If it is your intention then to share in the mystery, to share your laughter and your tears, your joys and your sorrows, and all that the years will bring to you both, let us go to the altar of our God, that you may bind yourselves to each other as husband and wife. Amen

— Jeffrey K. Kimpel
St. John's Lutheran Church
Fowlerville, Michigan

17

 A MARRIAGE MADE IN HEAVEN

(Readings: Isaiah 54:5-8; John 17:20-23)

A wedding is an occasion of great rejoicing. For ____ and ____ , this is a mature decision, based upon a relationship of many years standing. We rejoice with them as they enter together into the adventure of a lifetime.

The title of this sermon perhaps has you wondering how I can know that this marriage is "made in heaven." Well, as a matter of fact, I don't know that. How could anyone know that at this point? That's not to throw cold water on this joyous event, mind you. Actually, I had another marriage in mind in giving a title to this sermon — the marriage of Christ and the church. Now there's a marriage made in heaven, for it begins and ends with God's love.

Jesus alludes to this marriage in his high priestly prayer of John 17, where we read:

> *I do not pray for these only, but also for those who believe in me through their word, that they may all be one; even as you, Father, are in me, and I in you, that they also may be in us, so that the world may believe that you have sent me.*
> (John 17:20-21)

The intimacy of the relationship of Jesus and the Father is the cornerstone of Christ's marriage to the church — his very bride. That is why Christ emphasizes and prays for unity among all Christians. If Christians are one, the world will be more prone to see that Jesus and the Father are One. Conversely, if the church is divided, the witness of the church to the relationship of Christ and the Father will be hampered.

As many of you know, ____ and ____ come from differ-ent religious traditions. Nonetheless, they have been called to Holy Matrimony by the *one* Spirit that our respective churches share in common. For this reason, their marriage is a gift of the Spirit to the church, for it will stand as a bold image of our deeper unity in Christ, a unity that transcends the painful divisions within the body of Christ. They join an ever-growing number of interfaith marriages that are serving in subtle, but very real, ways to dissolve and heal our differences. Christ wants this — so that the world may believe.

The divisions that exist within the church should not be allowed to obscure what faith in God and participation in the church have to offer marriages. Despite its many flaws, the church is still the best place around for feeding and nourish-ing marriages at their deepest levels of need. Here are a few reasons why:

a. Christian faith confronts human sinfulness. It places a powerful check upon our tendency to blame others for problems that are essentially our own. Marriage puts us face-to-face with who we really are — warts and all. How healthy it is to be free to say to your husband or wife: "It's my fault; I'm sorry. Will you forgive me?"

b. Christian faith proclaims the dignity of each and every person as a child of God. Such a belief forms the basis for the respect that is essential to marriage. The persons to whom we are married are not someone that we own, nor are they something that we have earned, nor most assuredly are they something that we deserve. They are a gift — a sacred gift — of God.

c. Christian faith challenges us to put Christ at the center of all of our relationships, and most especially our marriages. Putting Christ at the center of a marriage changes the chemis-try entirely. Persons who are touched by God's grace them-selves become gracious. A marriage needs a whole bushel full of grace.

d. The Christian faith and life in the church teach patterns of openness, caring, and forgiving. These are qualities which, quite obviously, marriages need to survive.

The church, despite its many flaws, is still the best place for a marriage to be nourished and sustained at its deepest level of need. For a little bit of faith, you sure get a whole lot in return. God wants marriages to succeed. God wants those who enter into them to be happy, to be fulfilled, to be joyous. God wants our marriages to mirror the marriage that is made in heaven — the marriage of Christ to the church.

Folk wisdom holds that certain marriages are "made in heaven." This expression is often intended as a way of saying that a particular couple never had a disagreement, never had a stressful moment, never had a flash of anger or conflict for lo these many years. Maybe my experience is limited, but I've never known a marriage like that. As a matter of fact, I'm not so sure that I want to know a marriage like that; such a marriage may suffer from something even worse than conflict: boredom.

My theory is that a marriage "made in heaven" is one that is close to the love of God in Christ. Placing Christ at the center of your marriage will bear rich fruit over the years so that in hindsight, people will say of your marriage that it was, indeed, "made in heaven."

_____ and _____ , our prayer for you today is that you will build your marriage around the marriage that is made in heaven: the love of God in Christ for the church. Our prayer for you is that you will together seek out in freedom a community of Christians who will uphold your marriage and your faith in God. And lastly, our prayer for you is that someday your grandchildren will say to each other, when reflecting on the marriage of Grampa _____ and Gramma _____: "Ah yes, now *there* was a marriage made in heaven!"

God's peace to you. Amen

> — Craig Douglas Erickson
> Summit Avenue Presbyterian
> Church
> Bremerton, Washington

18

Yesterday was the Feast of Epiphany in the church's calendar — January sixth. The theme of Epiphany is the revealing of God in the lives of his people. The story we have just heard from John's Gospel, chapter two, is the text appointed for one of the Sundays of Epiphany. It is a story of how God revealed himself in a situation of life very much like the one in which we find ourselves now — a wedding. I like this story because it tells us many important things. I would like to share three of them with you now.

1. God is present in our celebrations. God wants you to be happy. That's the first point. It's a false notion that to be a Christian you can't have any fun. Those who boil Christianity down to a stiff legalism that allows no celebration have misunderstood our Lord's intentions.

So often we are like the farm boy whose grandma would not allow him to engage in what she called "worldly amusements" on Sundays — like playing baseball. Dejected and lonely, one Sunday afternoon he walked down to the barn and while he stood by the corral fence, a mule came up and put his head into the boy's hands. Patting the sad face of the mule, the boy said, "Poor fellow, you must be a Christian, too."

Christians have every reason to be the happiest people in the world, because Christ has forgiven their sins. Christ came to the wedding of this young couple in Cana of Galilee because God wants to be present in our celebrations.

2. God helps in our tribulation. If Jesus hadn't been there, he could not have helped them when they needed him. But he was a part of their celebration and that made all the difference for them. And that brings us to the second point of our story, God helps in our tribulations.

Like you, the young couple in our story thought, or at least they hoped, they had everything ready for the wedding. But an unexpected happening could have turned into one of life's most embarrassing moments. The wine ran out! In Jesus' day a wedding lasted from three days to a week. Relatives and friends came great distances to be there, and it was the responsibility of the wedding couple and their families to see that the needs of the guests were provided for. Wine was a usual part of the bill of fare. But in the middle of the wedding celebration they ran out of wine. For the couple this meant embarrassment in the least, if not disgrace.

What would you do if you were caught short? Seeing their plight, Jesus responded by supplying wine for the feast. You see, it's a good idea to have Jesus present in your marriage. In the unexpected moments of life, in your trials and tribulations, God's help will become real for you. He will be there when you need him. Just ask him.

3. God's goodness exceeds our expectations. Do you remember how it says, "When the steward of the feast tasted the water now become wine, he called the bridegroom and said, 'every man serves the good wine first . . . but you have kept the good wine until now' "?

The people got more than they bargained for. It was better than anybody could have expected. In our text, wine is a symbol of joy. It is also a symbol of God's grace which is abundant and overflowing. In his mercy, God has saved the best until last — the promise of salvation and eternal life.

It is wine that we receive in the Eucharist — the Holy Communion of Christ's blood — given and shed for you for the forgiveness of sins. It is wine, changed from water in our text, that stands for how your lives can be changed by the transforming love of God. _____ , _____ may the overflowing abundance of God's grace and love fill your lives with the wine of forgiveness so that you may be able to love and forgive one another as God forgives you.

We who are gathered here pray many blessings for you. We pray that you may remember that God wants to be a part of your *celebrations*, that he will always be there to help in your trials and *tribulations*, and that in his grace and abundant mercy he will always exceed your greatest *expectations*.

— Richard Kraiger
Bowman Lutheran Church
Bowman, North Dakota

19

I suppose the custom of playing innocent tricks on the bridal pair is universal. I don't know if you will get by without anything being done in a joking way on your wedding day, but I heard a story of one wedding where, as the bride and groom knelt before the altar for the vows, a restrained echo of giggling could be detected throughout the church. A member of the wedding party had painted in big white letters on the soles of the groom's shoes, the letters H E L P.

Now of course, when we speak about the theme of our text, "Our HELP is in the Name of the Lord," we do not mean it in the sense of the joke intended by the prankster who painted the word "help" on the soles of the groom. We are dead serious, when we say this afternoon to you, _____ and _____ , you need *Help to make a good marriage!*

1. "Help" may not be the usual things we think of when hearing a wedding address. We would go along with the idea that the very reason all our friends and family are present on this special day of _____ and _____ is to rejoice with them, to support them in their decision to begin life together as husband and wife. Our presence assures them that our prayers and good wishes accompany them as they, standing before God's altar, make their vows of faithfulness to each other and to their God.

But in our day and age, there is a tendency to go it alone. To consider oneself master of his/her own destiny. In marriage many try to do that very thing. They try to build a future of happiness on everything or anything except the "One Thing Needful." But the statistics of failure in marriage bear

71

out the fact that they are trying to build a home without the help they need most.

2. We need help. In life that is true. In moments of crisis, of decision, the wise person is thankful if there is a person to go to for advice, for help in whatever area of life that help may be needed.

And spiritually, that certainly is true. We are not self-made people. We are not masters of our own destinies. In fact, when it comes to our spiritual condition by nature, if we are honest with ourselves, we will have to admit that alone, we are in trouble. The Bible says, "The soul that sinneth it shall die." "The wages of sin is death." "There is not a just man on earth that doeth good and sinneth not."

Thankfully, in this respect, there is a way out. God is our very present helper. He loved us so much that he sent his own Son, "that whoever believes in him, should not perish, but have everlasting life." "He made him who knew no sin to be sin for us, that we might have the rightness of God in us." Good Friday testifies to the extent of that love for us. Easter seals it, and the Ascension of our Lord and Pentecost prove to us that we are not alone — that our God is very much alive, and with us, in the Word and Sacraments.

3. The words of Scripture before us say, "Our help is in the Name of the Lord who made heaven and earth."

Help is available to us in our gracious God. The same God who got us out of the greatest trouble known to man, the problem of our sin-filled hearts, promises to be present with us in all areas of life, including the task of building a new home.

The important thing is for us to recognize our need for help in this undertaking. Some have tried to go it alone, to trust in their own ability, in their bank account, in their own personalities. And yet, when the chips are down, when the wind blows, the problems arise, where is their help? "Our help is in the Name of the Lord!"

My hope and prayer for you, ____ and ____ , is that this will be your motto, your prayer from the very beginning of your marriage. Your love for each other is strong. And that is good. But remember how the devil works. He can change the picture from sunshine without a cloud in the sky to a real devastating blizzard.

Don't be too secure, too proud to admit your need of help. And remember our Lord's blessed promises, "Him that cometh to Me I will in no wise cast out." If you live in a relationship with Jesus as your Savior and constant Companion in good weather, when bad weather comes, you will not hesitate to say, "Our help is in the Name of the Lord." Amen

— Max Zschiegner
Hope Lutheran Church
Highland, Illinois

20

We have gathered here this day to witness a marriage. We will hear the promises that this man and woman will make to one another. They will be making a commitment. They will promise to love one another; to be faithful to one another; to be true to one another during good times as well as during bad times. The only thing that can break this commitment is death.

Does this sound frightening? Why in the world would anyone want to make such a commitment? No one knows what the future may hold. How can anyone make such promises not knowing what tomorrow will bring?

We all need someone to share our lives with; to share our hopes; our dreams; our disappointments with. There is a story told about a minister who just loved to play golf. One Sunday morning he arose to a beautiful day and decided to go golfing. He telephoned his council president and informed her that he was ill. He then took his golf clubs and headed for the golf course. St. Peter and St. John were looking down at this from heaven and they were upset by the pastor's behavior. "We must do something," shouted St. John. "Don't worry," said St. Peter. "I've got an idea." The first hole was a par 5, over 600 yards. The pastor teed up the ball, swung, and the ball sailed 600 yards, rolled up on the green, and went into the hole. "Why did you do that?" shouted St. John. "I thought you were going to punish him for playing golf instead of going to church!" "I did punish him," replied St. Peter. "He has just hit the greatest golf shot that golfer has ever hit, and whom is he going to tell?" The point of the story is that we

75

all need someone to share our lives with; that life has no meaning unless we have someone to share it with.

But why marriage? No one knows what the future may hold. It may bring fame and fortune. It may bring poverty and illness. Yet no matter what life may bring to us, we have someone with whom we can share our joys and sorrows; someone who is commited to us; someone whom we can count on; someone who we know cares about us.

How would you feel if marriage vows were conditional? You would never be sure when the other person might want to dissolve the marriage. You could become ill; your husband or wife might not desire to stay by you during such a circumstance.

But marriage is non-conditional. You still may become ill, but you know that you can count on your husband or wife to stand by you. This is one thing in life that you can count on. Why? Because that person has commited himself/herself to you. Don't you find that reassuring, knowing that you have someone who will stand beside you in life, someone you can share your life with? May you always remember the promises that you made to one another on this your wedding day. Amen

> — Paul N. Frank
> Trinity Evangelical
>   Lutheran Church
> Freeport, Pennsylvania